Hats Off to You, CHARLIE BROWN

IT SAYS HERE THAT IN BEETHOVEN'S TIME SOME CONCERTS LASTED FIVE OR SIX HOURS...

THINGS CHANGE, DON'T THEY? CONCERTS ARE GETTING SHORTER..

AND PAR-FIVES ARE GETTING LONGER

WHATEVER THAT MEANS

5-1

PEANUTS.

by SCHULZ

WHAT DO YOU HAVE THERE, SIR?

IT'S A GEMSTONE, MARCIE..A PIECE OF CRYSTAL!

IT'S GOING TO HELP GET ME PERFECT GRADES...

5-3

MY PERSONAL ELECTRICAL FIELD COMBINES WITH THE CRYSTAL'S ELECTROMAGNETIC FIELD! EASY, HUH? NO MORE STUDYING!

5-8

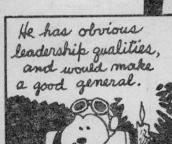

YES, MA'AM.. I FIX BREAKFAST FOR MYSELF AND FOR MY DAD EVERY MORNING...

HE NEVER REALLY WANTS MUCH..JUST SOME TOAST AND SOME COFFEE..DECAPITATED...

DECAFFEINATED!

WHATEVER..

5-18

PEANUTS
by SCHULZ

YOU KNOW, CHARLES, THIS TREE IS GOING TO GROW PRETTY HIGH IN THE NEXT FIFTEEN YEARS...

BY THE TIME YOU'RE OUT OF COLLEGE, YOU'LL BE TWENTY FEET IN THE AIR!

5-28

HOW AM I GOING TO GO TO COLLEGE IF I'M HANGING FROM A TREE?

MAYBE CORRESPONDENCE SCHOOL..

※ SIGH ※

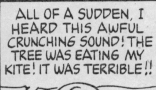

ON THIS TEST, MA'AM, DO YOU WANT OUR LAST NAME FIRST OR OUR FIRST NAME FIRST?

HOW ABOUT A MIDDLE INITIAL? SHOULD WE PUT DOWN A MIDDLE INITIAL?

OKAY, I GOTCHA..

NOT USED TO DEALING WITH A PERFECTIONIST, HUH, MA'AM?

PROOFREAD THIS FOR ME, WILL YOU, MARCIE?

I WANT TO BE SURE IT'S READY TO HAND IN...

6-8

IT'S PERFECT, SIR..

REALLY?

YOU MISSPELLED EVERY WORD!

Dear Contributor, We are returning your worthless story.

It is the dumbest story we have ever read.

Please don't send us any more. Please, Please, Please!

I LOVE TO HEAR AN EDITOR BEG..

6-11

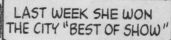

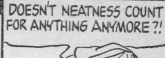

HEY, MANAGER.. I'VE BROUGHT MY ATTORNEY TO SEE YOU...

WE THINK I SHOULD GET PAID FOR PLAYING ON YOUR TEAM..

TELL YOUR ATTORNEY TO GET BACK AT SHORTSTOP WHERE HE BELONGS OR THERE'LL BE NO SUPPER TONIGHT!

I'VE NEVER SEEN AN ATTORNEY GIVE UP A CASE SO FAST...

PEANUTS.

by SCHULZ

Dear Dad, Thinking of you on Father's Day.

Yesterday I created a new recipe.

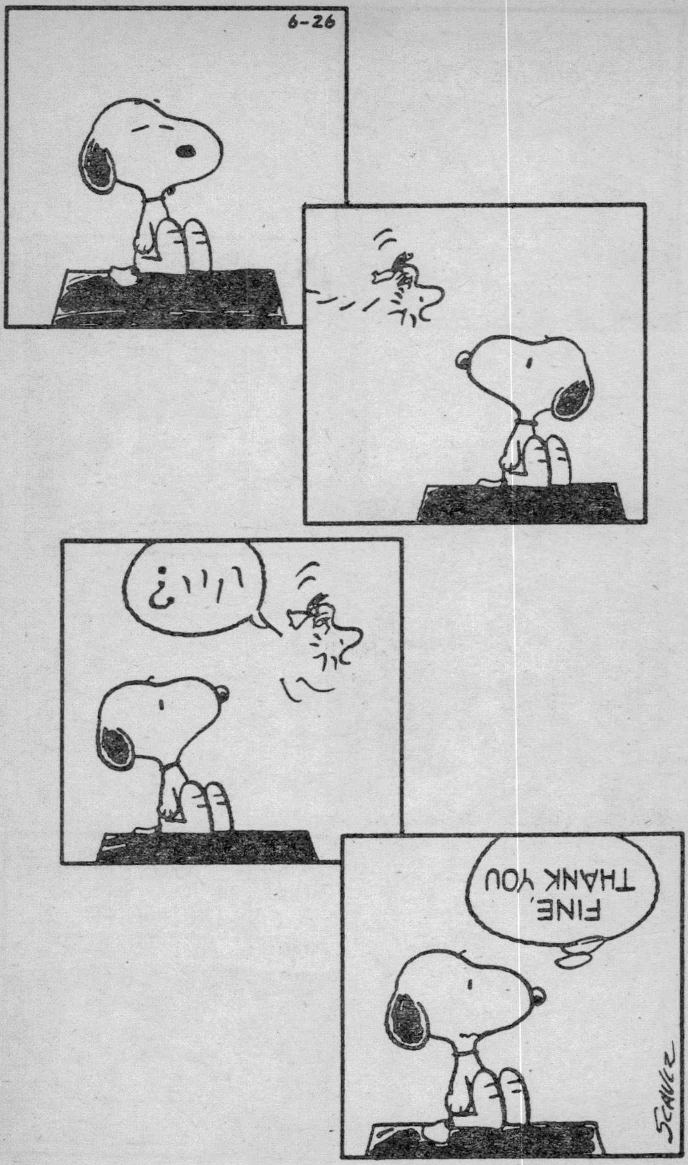
6-26
FINE, THANK YOU

6-29

HERE'S THE WORLD WAR I FLYING ACE SITTING IN A TINY FRENCH CAFE.. HE IS LONELY...

SUDDENLY, HE SEES A BEAUTIFUL FRENCH LASS AT THE NEXT TABLE...

SURE, WHAT WOULD YOU LIKE TO KNOW?

WELL, I'M SEVENTY-EIGHT YEARS OLD, AND THIS AFTERNOON I'M HAVING BYPASS SURGERY...

7-2

YOU'RE WELCOME

I DON'T HAVE TO GO TO SUMMER CAMP

I COULDN'T DECIDE IF I WANTED MARBLE FUDGE, CHOCOLATE, ROCKY ROAD, VANILLA OR BUTTER PECAN..

I FINALLY DECIDED TO TRY MARBLE FUDGE.. THEN I HAD TO CHOOSE BETWEEN A PLAIN CONE OR A SUGAR CONE...

7-3

I DECIDED ON THE SUGAR CONE..SO WHAT HAPPENED? I WENT OUT THE DOOR, AND DROPPED THE WHOLE THING ON THE SIDEWALK!

DON'T TELL ME MY LIFE ISN'T A SHAKESPEAREAN TRAGEDY..

I WON'T

HEY, MANAGER.. I BROUGHT YOU A LITTLE DRINK...

THAT'S VERY NICE OF YOU, BUT I REALLY DON'T CARE FOR LEATHER WATER..

7-4

"LEATHER WATER"?

WHAT DO YOU THINK IS THE BIGGEST PROBLEM WE HAVE TO WORRY ABOUT IN THE WORLD TODAY?

CHOCOLATE SUNDAES

THEY FILL UP THOSE TALL DISHES WITH THE ICE CREAM, RIGHT? THEN THEY POUR THE CHOCOLATE SAUCE OVER IT..

AS SOON AS YOU TRY TO DIG YOUR SPOON INTO THE ICE CREAM, THE CHOCOLATE RUNS OVER THE SIDE OF THE DISH..

THAT'S THE BIGGEST PROBLEM WE HAVE TO WORRY ABOUT IN THE WORLD TODAY

I JUST FOUND OUT WE'RE IN BETTER SHAPE THAN I THOUGHT WE WERE!

PEANUTS.
by SCHULZ

THIS LOOKS LIKE A GOOD SPOT..

I'LL GET THE LINE AND POLE READY.. YOU GET THE WORMS..

THAT WAS VERY EMBARRASSING, MARCIE..

WHY DID YOU HAVE TO TELL CHUCK THAT WE'D MISS HIM AND THAT WE LOVE HIM?

IT WAS THE TENDERNESS OF THE MOMENT, SIR.. KNOWING THAT WE WERE GOING OFF TO CAMP...

AND WE MAY NEVER SEE EACH OTHER AGAIN...

MARCIE!

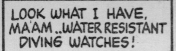

DID YOU KNOW THAT WOMEN CAN JOIN THE ROTARY CLUB NOW?

WHAT DO THEY DO AT ROTARY, SIR?

7-25

I THINK THEY HAVE LUNCH AND INSULT EACH OTHER..

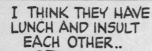

WE'D FIT RIGHT IN, WOULDN'T WE, SIR?

Panel 1: I'M GOING HOME TODAY, MA'AM..THANK YOU FOR THE SWIMMING LESSONS

Panel 2: YOU WERE A QUICK LEARNER, SOPHIE...

Panel 3: MAYBE YOU SHOULD TAKE BALLET LESSONS..

THAT'S A GOOD IDEA...

7-28

Panel 4: HERE I GO!!

8-6

A REAL RATTLESNAKE RATTLES HIS TAIL BEFORE STRIKING...

FLIP, FLOP, FLIP IS NOT RATTLING!

CATS ARE SO DUMB!

DID YOU EVER SEE A CAT SIT AND STARE AT A GOPHER HOLE?

THEY SIT THERE LIKE THIS, AND THEY JUST STARE...

BONK

SORRY, MANAGER, BUT ONE CAN'T EXPECT TO CATCH THEM ALL, CAN ONE?

WHEN ONE CONSIDERS HOW DIFFICULT IT REALLY IS, ONE MUST ADMIT THAT ONE IS FORTUNATE EVER TO CATCH THE BALL AT ALL, ISN'T ONE?

8-10

ONE WHO HAS YOU ON ONE'S TEAM IS FORTUNATE NOT TO LOSE ONE'S MIND, ISN'T ONE?!

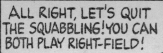

Copr. © 1952
United Feature Syndicate, Inc.

CHARLIE BROWN, SNOOPY and the whole PEANUTS® gang...

together again with another set of
daily trials and tribulations by

CHARLES M. SCHULZ